Volume 01

I0159594

INTIMATE
ENCOUNTERS

Communing with God and Becoming His Word

Zachary N. Taylor

madeforhisimage

ISBN-13: 978-0692169414 (madeforhisimage)

ISBN-10: 0692169415

Cover designed by zachtaylorstudios

Volume One

CONTENTS

INTRODUCTION

· ·

Pursuing and developing a deeper intimacy with our Heavenly Father is exactly where He wants us. In order to develop an intimate relationship with anyone, consistent and meaningful conversation must take place. One of the most powerful ways to commune with God is to embrace His Word on a personal level and begin to understand who He says we are and how much value He has placed on our lives.

It's one thing to read through the Scriptures, but for me they really came alive in my life when I personalized them and started speaking them back to my Father in more of a dialogue. During this time, God revealed to me that it is not only His will that I know His Word but rather become His Word. Going through the scriptures and embracing them as your identity is critical in becoming His word. Thank you for coming along side of me and embarking on this great adventure of knowing God and letting His Word become flesh in our lives.

Enjoy spending time with God as you go through these volumes and posture your heart to increase your intimacy with your Father and our Lord Jesus Christ. Many blessings to you!

GALATIANS

. . . .

Galatians 1

Father I thank you for giving me grace and peace through your Son Jesus Christ. Jesus thank you for shedding your blood for me. Thank you for giving yourself for my sins, delivering me from this evil age and establishing me inside of your Kingdom. Honor and glory be to your name forever and ever!

Father I thank you for calling me into your grace and keeping me from turning to another gospel. Not that there really is another gospel; however you have established me in your truth. Please continue to give me the wisdom to preach the true gospel you have given me. For I shall not seek the approval of man, but your approval is all that matters; for I am a servant of Jesus Christ my Lord.

Galatians 2

Father I thank you that I am not justified by my works but through faith in Jesus Christ my Lord. Thank you that justification only comes through Jesus and will never come through works of the law. You tore down my identity as a sinner and built me up as a son of God. Thank you that I have died to the law so that I can live unto You. Thank you that I have been crucified with Christ and it is no longer I who lives but Christ who lives in me. The life I now live in the flesh I live by faith in Your Son Jesus who loves me and gave His life for me. I shall not nullify the grace and sacrifice Jesus paid for me by seeking my righteousness through the law, because if it were so, then Jesus died for nothing.

Galatians 3

Father I thank you that I have received your Spirit by faith and not by works. Thank you that I am being perfected by the Spirit and not by my flesh. Thank you that by faith, you will continue to supply the Spirit and work out miracles in my life. By faith I am a son of God! I shall not fall under the curse of works of the law to establish my sonship; but rather by faith, I shall receive my sonship through Jesus Christ who became a curse for me and gave me His Spirit. Thank you I am now a son and an heir; no longer a slave to the law and to sin. Oh how could I ever turn back to that weak and worthless way of living according to the principles of this world? My slave days are over for I am a son! I am free!

Galatians 4

Father I thank you that you sent forth your Son, born of a woman and under the law so you could redeem me from the law and adopt me as a son. Thank you for making me a son and placing the Spirit of your Son in my heart which cries Abba! Father! Thank you I am no longer a slave but a son and an heir.

Father I thank you for revealing yourself to me and allowing me to know you and I'm thankful you know me! I am thankful I am no longer a slave to the weak and worthless principles of this world and I will never turn back to that slave mentality. Thank you that I am a son of promise born free according to the Spirit.

Galatians 5

Father I thank you that for freedom Christ has set me free! Thank you that I can stand firm and not ever submit to the yoke of slavery again. For I have been justified by your grace, not by the law; and through your Spirit, by faith, I shall obtain the hope of righteousness. For the only thing that really counts for anything in my life is faith working through love. I shall run well and not use my freedom as an opportunity to indulge the flesh but serve my brothers and sisters in love. For the whole law is summed up by "Loving my neighbor as myself."

Father I thank you that by walking in the Spirit, I shall not gratify the desires of my flesh. For the desires of my flesh are contrary to the Spirit. I shall not be led by the fruit of the flesh but rather be led by the fruit of the Spirit which is love, joy, peace, patience, kindness, goodness, faithfulness, gentleness, and self control. For my flesh has been crucified with Christ along with its passions and desires. If I live by the Spirit, then I shall walk by the Spirit!

Galatians 6

Father I thank you for giving me your Spirit so I can fulfill the law of Christ and love! Thank you that if I sow to the Spirit I shall reap things from the Spirit. I shall not sow to the flesh for I will only reap corruption from my flesh. I shall not grow weary in doing good, for in due season, I will reap the rewards as long as I don't give up. So then, as long as I have the opportunity to do so, I shall do good to everyone, especially to those in my household of faith. Thank you that I can only boast in the cross of my Lord Jesus Christ. He has crucified the world to me and me to the world. I am now a new creation; peace and mercy follow me everywhere I go for the grace of my Lord Jesus is with my spirit!

EPHESIANS

∙ ∙

Ephesians 1

Father I thank you for sending your Son and blessing me with Him as my Lord. In Him, you have given me every spiritual blessing. Thank you for choosing me to be in Christ; thinking of me even before you created the universe. Thank you for establishing my destiny to be holy and blameless in your sight. Because of your great love for me, you chose me to be adopted into your family as a son through Jesus Christ. I praise your glorious grace! Thank you for blessing me with Christ Jesus! In Him you gave me redemption through His blood and the forgiveness of my sins according to the riches of your grace that you lavished on me with all wisdom and understanding. You made known to me the mystery of your will, according to your will with which you set forth in Christ Jesus to unite all things in Him. Thank you that in Christ, I have received an inheritance of all things since you have predestined me to be united and one with Jesus Christ. All to the praise of your glory Father! Thank you for sealing me with your Holy

Spirit, who is the guarantee of my inheritance until that day I step into the fullness of everything you have given me.

Father I pray you will continue to give me a spirit of wisdom and more revelation in the knowledge of you and your glory; having the eyes of my heart enlightened, so that I will have complete hope to all that you have called me to; that I may have full understanding of the riches of your glorious inheritance in the saints, and the immeasurable greatness and power toward me because I believe. May I fully come to understand this power that is according to the working of your great might that worked as you rose Jesus from the dead and seated Him at Your right hand in the heavenly places far above all rule, authority, power, and dominion; far above every name that is named, not only in this age but in the age to come. Thank you for putting all things under the feet of Jesus and making Him head over all things to the church, which is His body, the fullness of Him who fills all in all!

Ephesians 2

Father I thank you I am no longer dead in my trespasses and the sins in which I once walked. Thank you I no longer follow the course of this world following the prince of the air, the spirit that is at work in the sons of disobedience among whom I once lived while in passionate pursuit of my flesh; carrying out the desires in my body and in my mind. I was by nature a child of wrath like the rest of mankind. But because You are rich in mercy and your great love for me, even when I was dead in my trespasses, you made me alive with Christ Jesus! By your grace I have been saved! You have raised me up and seated me in the heavenly places in Christ Jesus, so in the coming ages, You will show me the immeasurable riches of your grace and kindness toward me in Christ Jesus! For by your grace I have been saved through faith. This is not by my own doing; it was a gift from You so I cannot boast. Thank you that I am Your workmanship, created in Christ Jesus to do the good works which you already prepared for me to walk in.

Father I thank you that I am no longer separated from You and Jesus. Thank you that I am no longer alienated from Your glory or a stranger to your covenant; having no hope. But now by the blood of Christ Jesus I have been brought near and made one with You along with my brothers and sisters. I am now a fellow citizen and a member of Your household! Thank you for breaking down the walls of hostility found in the law and making peace with me through the blood of Christ. Thank you that I am being built together with my brethren into a holy temple with Jesus as the cornerstone! Thank you for taking up residence in me and creating me to be a holy dwelling place for You by the Spirit.

Ephesians 3

Father I thank you for making the mystery of Christ Jesus known to me by revelation, which was not made known to the sons of men in other generations as it has now been revealed to your holy apostles and prophets by the Spirit. This mystery is that as a Gentile, I am a fellow heir; member of the same body, and partaker of the promise in Christ Jesus through the gospel.

Father I thank you for making me a minister of the gospel according to the gift of your grace, which was given to me by the working of your power. To me, though I am the very least of all the saints, this grace was given, to preach to my fellow man the unsearchable riches of Christ, and to bring to light for everyone your plan of the mystery hidden for ages in Christ Jesus, who created all things, so that through the church Your manifold wisdom might now be made known to the rulers and authorities in the heavenly places. For this reason I bow my knees before you Father, from whom every family in heaven and on earth is named.

Father I thank you that according to the riches of your glory, you have granted me strength and power through your Spirit in my inner being, so that Christ may dwell in my heart through faith. Father thank you that I am rooted and grounded in love, and for giving me the strength to comprehend and know, with all the saints, the breadth, length, height, and depth of the love of Christ that surpasses knowledge, that I can be filled with all the fullness of God. Father I thank you that you are able to do abundantly more with my life than all I can ask, think or imagine; according to the power at work within me. Father

I give you all the honor and glory in the church and in Christ Jesus throughout all generations, forever and ever.

Ephesians 4

Holy Spirit help me to walk in a manner worthy of the calling to which I have been called. May I walk in humility, gentleness, and patience, bearing with one another in love, eager to maintain the unity of the Spirit in the bond of peace. There is one body and one Spirit—just as I was called to the one hope that belongs to my call— one Lord, one faith, one baptism, one God and Father of all, who is over all and through all and in all.

Father I thank you that grace was given to me according to the measure of Christ's gift. Therefore it says, "When he ascended on high he led a host of captives, and he gave gifts to men."(In saying, "He ascended," what does it mean but that he had also descended into the lower regions, the earth? He who descended is the one who also ascended far above all the heavens, that he might fill all things.)

Father I thank you for giving us apostles, prophets, evangelists, shepherds and teachers, to equip all the saints for the work of ministry, for building up the body of Christ, until we all attain to the unity of the faith and of the knowledge of the Son of God, to mature manhood, to the measure of the stature of the fullness of Christ, so that we may no longer be children, tossed to and fro by the waves and carried about by every wind of doctrine, by human cunning, by craftiness in deceitful schemes. Rather, speaking the truth in love, we are to grow up in every way into him who is the head, into Christ, from whom the whole body, joined and held together by every joint with which it is equipped, when each part is working properly, makes the body grow so that it builds itself up in love.

Father I thank you I no longer walk the way the world does, in the futility of their minds. I thank you I am no longer darkened in my understanding, alienated from the life of God because of the ignorance that is in the world, due to hardness of heart. Thank you that I am no longer callous and giving myself up to sensuality, greedy to practice every kind of impurity. Father I thank you that is not the way you taught me in Christ! Thank you for showing me the truth is in Jesus, to put off my old self, which belongs to my former manner of life and is corrupt through deceitful desires, and to be renewed in the spirit of my mind, and to put on the new self, created after the likeness of my Lord Jesus in true righteousness and holiness. Therefore having put away falsehood, I shall speak the truth with my neighbor, for we are members of one another. When I get angry I shall not sin or let the sun go down on my anger; giving no opportunity to the devil. I shall no longer be a thief and steal, but rather labor well doing honest work with my own hands, so that I may have something to share with anyone in need. No corrupting talk shall come out of my mouth, but only what is good for building up, as fits the occasion, that it may give grace to those who hear. I shall not grieve the Holy Spirit of God, by whom I was sealed for the day of redemption. I shall put away all bitterness, wrath, anger, clamor, slander, and malice but rather be kind, tenderhearted, and forgiving as God in Christ forgave me.

Ephesians 5

Father I thank you for creating me in your image; that as your beloved son I can grow up to be just like you. As your son, I shall walk in love, just as Christ loved me and gave himself up for me, as a fragrant offering and sacrifice to our Father.

Father I thank you that sexual immorality, impurity, covetousness, filthiness, foolish talk, and crude joking are no longer a part of who I am; but instead I shall live in a posture of thanksgiving. Father I thank you for purifying my heart and giving me my inheritance in the kingdom of Christ Jesus. I shall not be deceived by empty words, for because of impurity, your wrath will come upon the sons of disobedience. Therefore I shall not become partners with them; for at one time I walked in darkness, but now I am light in the Lord. I shall walk as a child of light (for the fruit of light is found in all that is good and right and true), and I shall discern what is pleasing to my Lord. I shall take no part in the unfruitful works of darkness, but instead expose them. For it is shameful even to speak of the evil things that are done in secret. But when anything is exposed by the light, it becomes visible, for anything that becomes visible is light. Therefore it says, "Awake, O sleeper, and arise from the dead, and Christ will shine on you." I shall pay careful attention as to how I walk, not as unwise but as wise, making the best use of my time, because the days are evil. I shall not live foolish, but understand what your will for my life is. I shall not get drunk with wine, for that is debauchery, but I shall be filled with the Spirit, addressing my brethren in psalms, hymns and spiritual songs, singing and making melody to you Lord with my heart, giving thanks always for everything you have done in me in the name of my Lord Jesus Christ, and submitting to my brethren out of reverence for Jesus Christ my Lord.

Father I thank you for creating husband and wife in your image as a perfect representation of our oneness and intimacy with you. Thank you for showing us how to submit to each other in reverence to our Lord Jesus.

Father I thank you for creating me as a husband to love my wife, just as Christ loved the church and gave himself up for her, that he might sanctify her, having cleansed her by the washing of water with the word, so that he might present the church to himself in splendor, without spot or wrinkle or any such thing, that she might be holy and without blemish. I thank you that in the same way, I shall love my wife as my own body; for he who loves his wife loves himself. For no one ever hated his own flesh, but nourishes and cherishes it, just as Christ does the church, because we are members of your body. "Therefore a man shall leave his father and mother and hold fast to his wife, and the two shall become one flesh." This mystery is profound, and it refers to Christ and the church, just as each husband shall love his wife as himself, and each wife shall respect her husband.

Ephesians 6

Father I thank you for creating your children in your image and as your children we obey our parents in the Lord, for this is right. "Honor your father and mother" (this is the first commandment with a promise), "that it may go well with you and that you may live long in the land." I thank you for creating Fathers in your image and as you are so are we, not provoking our children to anger, but bringing them up in the discipline and instruction of the Lord.

Father I thank you that we get to display your image everywhere we go to include the situations where we come under the authority of another. I shall learn to obey these authorities with fear and trembling, with a sincere heart, as I would Christ, not by the way of eye-service, as people-pleasers, but as a bondservant of Christ, doing your will from a sincere heart, rendering service with a good will as to you Lord and not to man, knowing that whatever good I do, I shall receive back from you Lord. Father I thank you that as I am in a position of authority, I shall do the same and not be threatening, knowing that he who is both their Master and mine is in heaven, and that there is no partiality with You.

Father, I thank you that in you I find my strength and I shall continue to grow and walk in the strength of your might. Thank you for clothing me in your mighty armor so that I am able to stand against the schemes of the devil. For my war is not against flesh and blood, but against the rulers, against the authorities, against the cosmic powers over this present darkness, against the spiritual forces of evil in the heavenly places. Therefore I shall utilize all the armor you have given me, so that I will withstand these evil days, and having done all, I shall continue to stand firm. Therefore I shall stand, having fastened on the belt of truth, and having put on the breastplate of righteousness, and, as shoes for my feet, having put on the readiness given by the gospel of peace. In all circumstances I shall take up the shield of faith, with which I can extinguish all the flaming darts of the evil one; and take the helmet of salvation, and the sword of the Spirit, which is your Word, praying at all times in the Spirit, with all prayer and supplication. All the way until the end, I shall keep alert with all perseverance, making supplication for all the saints, and also for me, that words may be given to me in opening my mouth boldly to proclaim the mystery of the gospel, for which you have made me an ambassador, that I may declare it boldly, as I ought to speak.

PHILIPPIANS

. . . .

Philippians 1

Father I thank you for my partnership in the gospel and knowing the good work you started within me will continue to completion; for I am a partaker of the grace that is found in Christ Jesus. Father may your grace continue to transform me and show me how to abound more and more in love, knowledge, and discernment, so that I may approve of your most excellent ways; keeping me pure and blameless for the day of the Lord Jesus. Father for your glory, continue to fill me with the fruit of righteousness that comes through knowing You and my Lord Jesus Christ.

Father I thank you the the trials of my life are served to advance the gospel and to encourage my brothers and sisters all the more to speak the word more boldly and without fear. Thank you for teaching me to preach Christ out of sincere love and good will and not out of envy or rivalry; giving Christ full honor within this body. Thank you for this life and the understanding that to live is Christ and to die is gain. For as long as I am in this body, I will produce good fruit and be an encouragement for those around me; giving joy in the faith and glory to my Lord Jesus Christ.

Father I thank you for teaching me to live my life in a manner worthy of the gospel of Christ, standing firm for the gospel, and striving side by side with my brothers and sisters in one spirt and one mind without fear. Father thank you that your salvation allows me to persevere through the same sufferings as my Lord Jesus and ultimately serves to advance the gospel.

Philippians 2

Father I thank you that in you I find encouragement, comfort, love, affection, and sympathy and get to participate in these qualities of yours in the Spirit. Thank you for teaching me humility and showing me this life you have given me is not about me but rather bringing glory to your name, and becoming love, so I can see others as more significant than myself; looking after their interests above my own. Thank you for giving me Christ Jesus my Lord as an example of this humility, exalting His name above every name, allowing me to confess Jesus is Lord, and bowing to His name.

Father I thank you for working in me what is pleasing to you and showing me your will. Thank you that in all circumstances I can do everything without grumbling or complaining as an innocent child of God. Thank you for cleansing me and seeing me without blemish in the midst of a crooked and twisted generation; allowing me to shine as a light in this world as I hold fast to your word which gives life so that I may stand proud in the presence of my Lord Jesus Christ.

Father I thank you for giving me a genuine concern for the welfare of my brothers and sisters. Thank you for teaching me to put my own interests aside and seeking the interests of my Lord Jesus; serving the gospel as a brother, son, minister, messenger, and soldier.

Philippians 3

Father I thank you I do not have to create my own righteousness and put confidence in my flesh. For my confidence comes from my Lord Jesus and I shall worship Him by the Spirit. Father I lay my rights down and count my life as nothing; counting everything as loss compared to the surpassing worth of knowing my Lord Jesus Christ. I lay everything at the feet of Jesus and count it all as nothing for I gain everything in my Lord Jesus; for by faith His righteousness becomes my righteousness. Father I thank you that through faith in Christ's righteousness, I get to know Him, partake in the power of His resurrection, share in His sufferings, and become like him in his death; obtaining resurrection from the dead.

Jesus I thank you for making me your own and giving me your Spirit so I can forget everything behind me and continue to press forward to everything that lies ahead of me. Father I thank you for showing me how to think with maturity and I shall press on toward the goal for the prize of the upward call of God in Christ Jesus. Thank you for placing people in my life I can learn from who walk according to the example you have given us in Christ and the Apostles. Thank you that my citizenship is in heaven so I can set my thoughts not on earthly things but rather on heavenly things as I wait for my Savior, the Lord Jesus to transform my lowly body to be like His glorious body by the power that enabled Him to subject all things to Himself.

Philippians 4

Father I thank you for placing my name in the book of life. I shall rejoice in the Lord always, yes I shall rejoice! Father I thank you I do not have to worry about anything but rather by prayer and supplication I can let my requests be known to you with a heart of thankfulness. Father I thank you that your peace which surpasses all understanding will guard my heart and mind in Christ Jesus.

Father I thank you for filling my mind with truth and what is honorable, just, pure, lovely, commendable, excellent, and worthy of praise; for your peace will always be with me. Father I thank you for showing me how I can be content in all stages of life. I can remain steadfast in times of being brought down low and times of abundance. In each and every circumstance you have taught me the secret of facing plenty and hunger, abundance and need; I can do all things though Christ who strengthens me and knowing you shall supply every need of mine according to the riches that are in the glory of Christ Jesus. Father glory to your name for ever and ever!

Volume One

COLOSSIANS

. . . .

Colossians 1

Father I thank you for faith in my Lord Jesus Christ; teaching me how to love and how to hold on to the hope laid out before me. Father I thank you that the power of the gospel of truth is bearing more and more fruit in my life as I continue to understand your grace more and more. Father, I ask you to continue filling me with the knowledge of your will with all spiritual wisdom and understanding so I may always walk in a pleasing manner worthy of my Lord; always bearing fruit in every good work and forever increasing in knowing you.

Father I thank you that as I continue to know you more intimately, you will continue to strengthen me with more of your power; strengthening my endurance, patience, joy, and thanksgiving. Father I thank you for qualifying me to possess my inheritance along with my brothers and sisters in Christ and filling us with your light; having delivered us from the domain of darkness and transferring us into the Kingdom of your beloved Son, in whom we have redemption and the forgiveness of our sins.

Father I thank you for giving me Your Son Jesus, the firstborn of all creation, in order to put your image on full display. Jesus, thank you for your creation; for there was nothing on this earth or in heaven made apart from your hands. Everything my eyes can see and can't see was made by you and for you; for you eternally existed before all these things and hold them all together with the power of your hand. Father I thank you for making Jesus the preeminent head of your body, the church, for He is the firstborn from the dead.

Father I thank you that it pleased you to put the fullness of who you are in Christ and make yourself known to me. Jesus thank you for reconciling me back to my Father and making peace with me through the blood you shed for me on the cross. Father I thank you that even though I was once alienated and hostile in mind toward you; doing all kinds of evil deeds, you never lost site of who you created me to be and therefore reconciled me in the body of Christ through His death and now I stand holy, blameless, and above reproach in your site. Father I thank you that your truth and identity has set me so free, I could never turn away from my faith in the finished work of the cross, and I shall continue to remain stable and steadfast; never shifting from the hope that lies in the gospel.

Father I thank you I can actually rejoice in my sufferings for the sake of the gospel which you have made me a minister of, according to the free gift you have given me, so that I can make your Word known. Father I thank you for revealing to me the mystery that was hidden for ages and generations which is Christ in me the hope of glory. For the hope of you receiving glory on this earth lies with my understanding that Christ lives in me. Father I ask you to continue maturing me in this understanding so I can warn, teach, and proclaim this truth with all wisdom and understanding so that everyone you lead me to can also be presented mature in Christ bringing you glory.

Colossians 2

Father I thank you for encouraging my heart and giving me riches of full assurance of understanding and knowledge of your mystery found in Christ which is where all the treasures of wisdom and knowledge exist. Thank you for making this wisdom and knowledge found in Christ known to me so that I will never run after plausible arguments against anything other than standing firm in the faith in my Lord Jesus Christ.

Father I thank you for Christ Jesus and I receive Him with thanksgiving! Being rooted and built up in the faith I shall walk in Him and never be taken captive by empty philosophies or deceit according to human traditions or elemental spirits of this world.

Father I thank you that the fullness of who you are dwells in Christ and you have filled me with Him who is the head of all rule and authority. Father thank you for giving me a circumcision of my flesh, not done with humans hands, but by putting off my body of flesh in Christ Jesus; having been buried with him in baptism and raised with him through faith in your powerful working which raised Him from the dead. For I was once dead in my trespasses and the uncircumcision of my flesh, but you made me come alive within my Lord Jesus, forgiving all my trespasses and canceling my record of debt that stood with its legal demands. Father thank you for taking these trespasses and nailing them to the cross and disarming the rulers and authorities; putting them to open shame, and triumphing over them for ever! Father I thank you that in Christ, I have died to the elemental spirits of this world and no longer live a sensual life pursuing the flesh. I shall hold fast to the Head, Christ Jesus, which the whole body is nourished and knit together though its joints and ligaments, growing as you cause and will.

Colossians 3

Father I thank you that I have been raised to life with Christ who is seated at your right hand. Being found in Christ I shall set my mind on things that are above, not on things that are on the earth; for I died and my life is hidden in Christ, and when he appears, I shall also appear with Him in glory. Father I thank you for putting to death what is earthly in me: sexual immorality, impurity, lust, evil desire, covetousness, and idolatry. Father I thank you I no longer walk in this manner and your wrath is no longer upon me for I have put off anger, wrath, malice, slander, and obscene talk from my mouth. Father I thank you lies are no longer on my lips for I have put off the old self with all its evil practices and have put on the new self which you have renewed in knowledge after the image of my Creator; Christ Jesus! As your chosen one, holy and beloved, I shall put on a compassionate heart, being kind, humble, meek, and patient; bearing with others and forgiving. Above all else I shall put on love which binds all of these things together in perfect harmony and allow the peace of Christ to rule in my heart. Father I thank you for giving me your word and allowing it to dwell in my heart, richly teaching and admonishing me with wisdom and thankfulness. Father I thank you that whatever I do, either in word or deed, I can do it in the name of my Lord Jesus, always giving thanks to you Father.

Father I thank you for modeling the family after yourself. I thank you for showing us how to submit to each other and showing us how to love each other like Christ. I thank you for giving me the work I have and the ability to do it with integrity as if I'm working for the Lord. I thank you for teaching me the goal is not to be a people-pleaser but rather with sincerity of heart, to give the Lord my best effort and allow Him to reward me.

Colossians 4

Father I thank you for entrusting me with the ability to follow and to lead; always following your example set in Christ, being just and fair in all I do. Father I thank you for opening up the lines of communication with me and allowing me to remain steadfast and watchful in prayer; always maintaining a thankful heart.

Father I ask you to continue opening doors to share your Word and declare the mystery of Christ. Father I ask you to help me make your Word clear so that I may speak with wisdom and make the best use of the time you have given me. May my speech be gracious and seasoned with salt, so that I may know how to speak to anyone. Father I thank you for maturing me, allowing me to stand fully assured of your will, and the grace to fulfill the ministry you have given me.

1 TIMOTHY

....

1 Timothy 1

Father, thank you for helping me to properly steward my faith as I aim at becoming love which stems from a pure heart, a good conscience, and a sincere faith. Jesus I thank you for giving me your strength, judging me faithful, and allowing me to serve your gospel even though I used to walk contrary to everything you came to destroy. Father thank you for pouring out your mercy upon me and not holding my ignorance of unbelief against me. Jesus thank you for pouring your grace, faith and love upon me and saving me from my wretched sinfulness. Thank you for pouring out mercy upon me so my life can reflect your perfect character and set an example for those who may believe in you and inherit eternal life. I praise you Jesus; the King of all ages, the invisible only God be honor and glory forever and ever!

1 Timothy 2

Father I thank you for guiding me into the truths and power of supplications, prayer, intercession, and thanksgiving. I lift up our leaders in this country and pray for dignified godly leadership to flow forth. I thank you that it is your will that all men come to the knowledge of truth and be saved. Thank you Jesus for giving up your life and becoming the mediator between my Father and I. Holy Spirit, continue to empower me to preach these truths and give me influence everywhere I place my feet; lifting holy hands without anger or quarreling.

1 Timothy 3

Father I thank you you are calling me to tend to your sheep. Continue to refine me with the type of character that would qualify me to lead your people well. Thank you that you have called your church to represent and be the pillar of truth in this world. Thank you that you will keep me in your truth and I shall not depart from the faith or devote my life to lies from the enemy. I shall not have anything to do with irreverent silly myths but rather devote myself to your truth and train myself for godliness. I shall toil and strive toward this goal because I have my hope set on you, the living God, who is my Savior. Thank you that I get to set the example in speech, conduct, love, faith, and purity. Father give me the desire and gifts to exhort and teach your holy Word. Give me influence to speak your truths into people's lives. May I be sincere and devoted to this high calling and continue to grow in truth.

1 Timothy 4

Father I thank you for keeping me in the truth of your Word and building my faith with sincerity of heart. I shall not depart from the Spirit of truth and follow deceitful spirits or demonic teachings. Father I thank you for giving me a clean conscious and I receive all you have given me with thanksgiving. Father I thank you for training me in godliness and showing me the ignorance of following irreverent silly myths, for my hope is set on you only, the one and only true living God; my Savior! Holy Spirit continue to empower me to teach these things with authority and be an example to follow; giving full attention to the public reading of Scripture, exhortation, and teaching. Father I shall not neglect the gifts you have given me, for I shall immerse myself in them and perfect them with persistence.

1 Timothy 5

Father I thank you for my family and my family of believers. Continue to show me how to care for, love, and encourage my brothers and sisters in the Lord. Thank you for giving us elders in the church and showing us how to honor and respect them as they honor you in the ministries you have given them. Father anoint these elders to teach and preach with bold confidence and supply all their needs to continue spreading the gospel.

1 Timothy 6

Father I thank you for sealing true doctrine in my mind and heart that agrees with the sound words of my Lord Jesus Christ. Teach me how to be godly and not puffed up with conceit. Father fuel my desire to always want a healthy craving for truth not controversy. Keep me from quarreling about words which produce envy, dissension, slander, evil suspicions, and constant friction among people. I want to be full of the truth, not deprived of truth trying to achieve earthly gain through godliness. I thank you that there is gain in godliness with contentment. Continue to teach me how to be content while I trust in you to provide for my real needs. Keep me from falling into the temptations of striving to achieve earthly riches and straying from the truth that leads to godliness. I shall flee from these things and pursue righteousness, godliness, faith, love, steadfastness, and gentleness. I shall fight the good fight of faith and take hold of the eternal life to which I have been called. I shall not set my hopes on the uncertainty of riches but on You who richly provides me with everything to enjoy. Father, my desire is to be rich in good works, generous, and ready to share; therefore storing up treasure as a good foundation for the future so I can take hold of what is truly life.

2 TIMOTHY

....

2 Timothy 1

Father I thank you for a clean conscience and a sincere faith filled with joy. My heart is to fan into flame the gifts you have and will continue to give me. May I burn brightly, for you have not given me a spirit of fear; but of power, love, and self-control. Therefore I shall not be ashamed of the gospel, but take comfort in suffering for the sake of the gospel in the power of the Holy Spirit. Father you saved me and called me to a holy calling, not because of my works but because of your own purpose and grace which you gave me in Christ Jesus before the ages even began. My purpose was made manifest at the coming of my Lord Jesus Christ who abolished death and brought life and immortality to light through the gospel. Father continue to fill me with your will and empower me to teach and preach your gospel. I shall never stand ashamed for I have put my faith in you and I am convinced that you will guard what you have entrusted to me until that Day. I shall follow the pattern of your word along with the faith and love that is in

Christ Jesus, empowered by the Holy Spirit who dwells within me; guarding the good deposit you entrusted to me.

2 Timothy 2

Jesus thank you for strengthening me in your grace and the ability to proclaim your word to faithful men who in turn will also proclaim your word. Father I shall share in sufferings as a good soldier of Christ Jesus, not getting entangled by the civilian affairs of this world, but be readily engaged in your army of love. Your word will not be bound so I shall endure everything thrown at me for the sake of my brethren that your salvation and glory may dwell in the hearts of man. In you I have died, so I can live. I shall always endure, so I can reign with you. I will not deny you as you will not deny me. I shall not get into quarreling about words for it does no good and only ruins those who hear it.

Father I thank you I stand before you as one approved, not ashamed, rightly handling your word of truth. I shall avoid irreverent babble for it only leads people into ungodliness and spreads like gangrene. I shall stand on the firm foundation; bearing the seal of sonship. For you know that I belong to you and as my Father and Lord, I shall depart from inequity and walk as a son of the Most High who has been set apart for His Fathers holy and honorable use; ready for every good work. Therefore I shall flee from youthful lusts and pursue righteousness, faith, love, and peace, along with those who call on the Lord with a pure heart. I shall not be quarrelsome, but kind to everyone, able to teach, patiently enduring evil, correcting those against me with love, patience, and gentleness; for You may grant them repentance leading to knowledge of the truth, and escape the snare of doing the devil's will.

2 Timothy 3

Father, I thank you for teaching me the power of godliness and how to follow truth and the way of faith, patience, love, and steadfastness. Persecutions and sufferings will come, but this will not derail me from living a godly life in Christ Jesus. I shall continue in what I have learned and firmly believe knowing that I come from you. Thank you for giving me your Word which I can use for teaching, rebuking, correction, and training in righteousness, so that being a child of God, I can be competent and equipped for every good work.

2 Timothy 4

Father I thank you for charging me with the honor of preaching your word. I shall be ready in season and out of season. I shall reprove, rebuke, and exhort with complete patience and teaching. For I understand the time is nearly approaching that people will not listen to sound teaching, but having itching ears, they will accumulate for themselves teachers to suit their passions and will turn from listening to the truth. I shall be sober minded, endure suffering, do the work of an evangelist, and fulfill my ministry. When the end of this race comes I may stand firm knowing I have finished well, fought the good fight, and kept the faith; henceforth awaiting me the crown of righteousness which my Lord and righteous judge will reward to me on that Day.

TITUS

....

Titus 1

Father I thank you for the gift of faith and granting me salvation. Thank you for showing me knowledge of the truth of godliness found in the word of Christ and showing me the power of hope found in your promise of eternal life.

Titus 2

Father thank you for teaching me to be self-controlled. Father thank you for establishing me as a model of good works, integrity, dignity, and sound speech that cannot be condemned. For your grace has come to bring me salvation and train me to renounce ungodliness and worldly passions. Your grace allows me to live a self-controlled, upright, and godly life as I await my blessed hope of seeing King Jesus return in glory. Jesus thank you for giving yourself for me, to redeem me from all lawlessness, and to purify me for your our own possession in which I have become zealous for good works.

Father thank you for calling me to be submissive to authority, and to be obedient and ready for every good work. Thank you for showing me to speak evil of no one, to avoid quarreling, to be gentle, and to show perfect courtesy toward all people. I was once a very foolish person who was led astray and disobedient. I was a slave to my internal passions and external pleasures. Malice and envy was in my heart while hating and being hated by others. But when your goodness and loving kindness appeared, you saved me. Not because of any works done by me but according to your mercy. Father thank you for washing me clean, regenerating my heart, and renewing me in your Holy Spirit; whom you richly poured out upon me through Jesus Christ my Savior, so that being justified by your grace I may become an heir according to the hope of eternal life. As an heir, I shall devote myself to good works so my life may profit the people around me and not be led into worthless things like controversy, divisions, quarreling, or dissension; for these ways of life are warped, sinful and self-condemning.

PHILEMON

. . . .

Philemon

Father, I pray that as I continue to know you better that I be known for the love and faith that I have toward the Lord Jesus and for all your saints, and I pray that the sharing of my faith may become effective for the full knowledge of every good thing that is in me for the sake of Christ. For I hope to impart much joy and comfort from your love to my brothers and sisters, because my heart is continually refreshed through you.

madeforhisimage

www.ingramcontent.com/pod-product-compliance
Lightning Source LLC
Chambersburg PA
CBHW060629030426
42337CB00018B/3274